GIANT VEHICLES
An Imagination Library Series

GIANT DUMPTRUCKS

Jim Mezzanotte

GARETH**STEVENS**
GS
PUBLISHING
A Member of the WRC Media Family of Companies

Please visit our web site at: **www.garethstevens.com**
For a free color catalog describing Gareth Stevens Publishing's list of high-quality books
and multimedia programs, call 1-800-542-2595 (USA) or 1-800-387-3178 (Canada).
Gareth Stevens Publishing's fax: (414) 332-3567.

Library of Congress Cataloging-in-Publication Data

Mezzanotte, Jim.
    Giant dump trucks / by Jim Mezzanotte.
       p. cm. — (Giant vehicles)
    Includes bibliographical references and index.
    ISBN 0-8368-4912-4 (lib. bdg.)
    ISBN 0-8368-4919-1 (softcover)
    1. Dump trucks—Juvenile literature.   I. Title.
  TL230.15.M48   2005
  629.225—dc22   2005045154

First published in 2006 by
Gareth Stevens Publishing
A Member of the WRC Media Family of Companies
330 West Olive Street, Suite 100
Milwaukee, WI 53212 USA

Editorial direction: Mark J. Sachner
Editor: JoAnn Early Macken
Art direction: Tammy West
Cover design and page layout: Kami M. Koenig
Photo editor: Diane Laska-Swanke
Picture researcher: Martin Levick

Photo credits: Cover, pp. 5, 7, 15, 17, 19, 21 © Eric Orlemann; pp. 9, 13 Courtesy of Liebherr Mining Equipment Co.;
p. 11 Courtesy of Komatsu America Corp.

Printed in the United States of America

1 2 3 4 5 6 7 8 9 09 08 07 06 05

COVER: A giant dump truck is
taller than some buildings!

Table of Contents

The Biggest Trucks 4

Bigger and Better 6

How Big Is Big? 8

Big Power 10

A Big Bed 12

Inside the Cab 14

At Work 16

Behind the Wheel 18

Truck Makers 20

More to Read and View 22

Web Sites 23

Glossary and Index 24

Words that appear in the glossary are printed in

The Biggest Trucks

Some dump trucks are huge. They are bigger than many buildings. They are called off-highway trucks. They are the biggest trucks in the world.

These trucks mostly work at **mines**. At mines, big machines dig for **coal** and other things. The trucks carry away the machine's big loads of earth.

A giant dump truck is too big for regular roads. The truck goes to a mine in pieces. At the mine, it is put together. Huge dump trucks are strong and powerful. The trucks work every day of the year. They even work at night. They never stop working!

At a mine, a shovel fills a giant dump truck. This truck was made by Caterpillar. After it unloads, it goes right back for more.

Bigger and Better

Many years ago, there were no giant dump trucks. People had to use regular trucks. They **modified** the trucks to make them stronger. But the trucks were still not strong enough. They were also too small. Machines for digging improved. They could dig huge amounts. The trucks could not keep up!

Off-highways trucks were first made in the 1930s. They were bigger than ordinary trucks. They were stronger, too. They could haul huge loads. The first big trucks for mines were built in the 1950s.

Over the years, digging machines got even bigger. Dump trucks got bigger, too. Bigger trucks can haul more in fewer trips. By the 1970s, these trucks were huge!

The Euclid company made this truck in the 1950s. It used to be the world's biggest dump truck. Today, giant trucks are much larger!

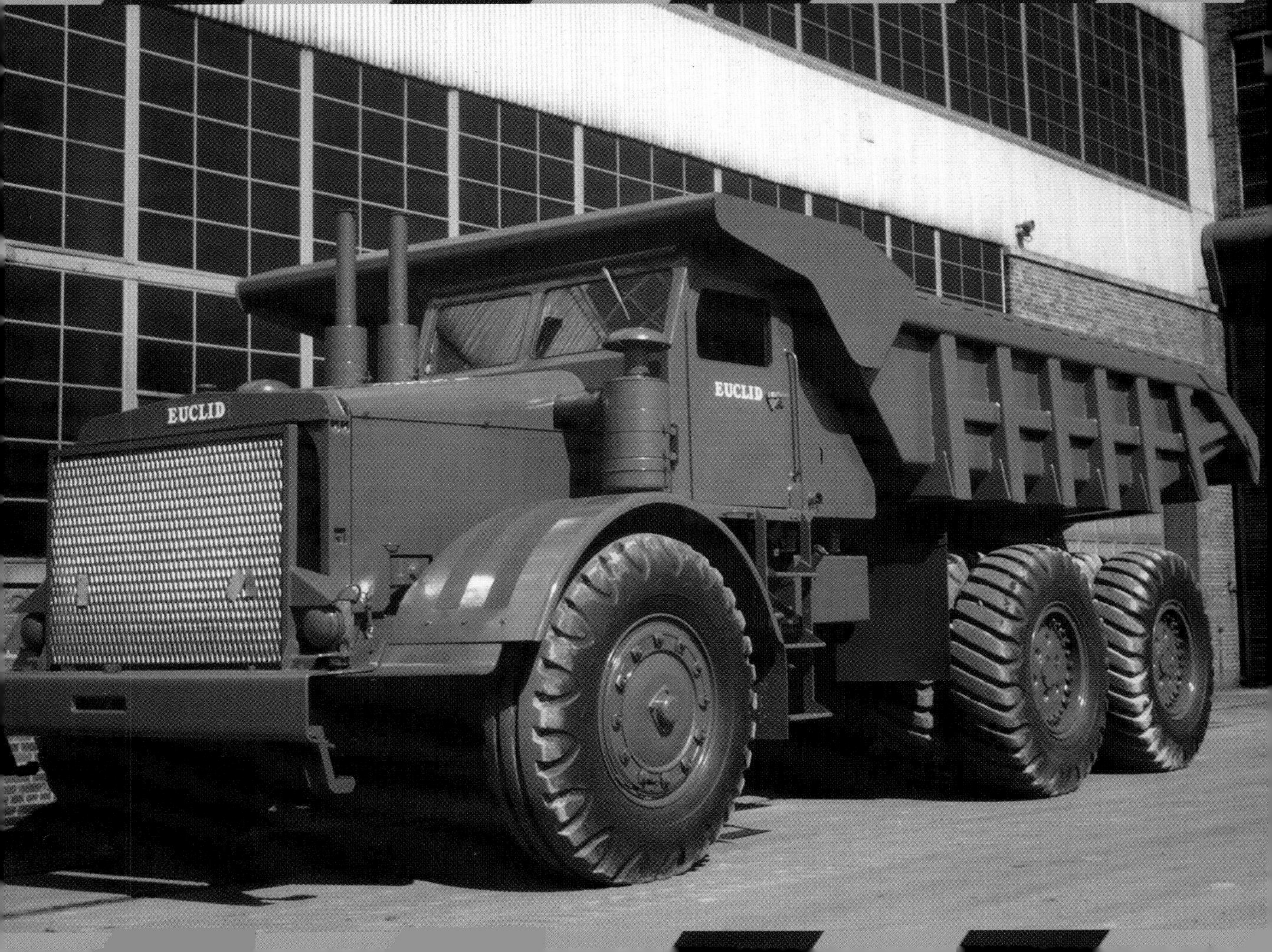
EUCLID
EUCLID

How Big Is Big?

Most cars weigh less than 3 tons. Today, a giant dump truck carries a load that weighs more than 300 tons. With a big load, the truck can weigh one million pounds! You could park many cars in the dump truck's **bed**.

The engine weighs many times more than a car. A single tire does, too! The tires are twice as high as an adult person. Most cars hold less than 20 gallons (75 liters) of **fuel**. A giant dump truck holds more than 1,000 gallons (3,785 l) of fuel!

A giant dump truck is taller than a two-story building. Drivers sit 20 feet (6 meters) up in the air. They get to the cab by climbing a long stairway.

The driver seems tiny next to this giant truck. He has to climb stairs to reach the driver's seat. This truck was made by Liebherr.

Big Power

Giant dump trucks have huge, powerful engines. Most car engines have four or six **cylinders**. Giant truck engines can have up to twenty cylinders. Some have even more! These engines are **diesel** engines, not gas engines. They use diesel fuel.

The engines make a lot of **horsepower**. Most car engines make less than 200 horsepower. Some giant truck engines make more than 3,500 horsepower! They use **turbochargers** for more power. Huge **radiators** keep them cool.

In some giant trucks, the engine turns the wheels. Other giant trucks work differently. Their engines create power for electric motors. These motors turn the wheels.

Giant trucks move heavy loads. This truck was made by Komatsu. Electric motors turn its wheels.

A Big Bed

The bed in a giant dump truck is very tough. It is made of steel. The steel is almost 1 inch (2.5 centimeters) thick. The bed usually has a V shape. This shape keeps the load down low so the truck will not tip over. The bed has a shelf in front over the cab. The shelf protects the driver.

Giant dump trucks unload just like smaller ones. The bed tilts up, and the load slides out. The bed is flat and smooth for better sliding.

Big **hydraulic** cylinders are attached to the bed. The cylinders tilt the bed. The cylinders are tubes. They have smaller tubes inside. These tubes are called pistons. Pumps force the oil up inside the cylinder. The oil pushes the pistons. The pistons are now longer. They rise up to lift the bed.

This Liebherr truck is unloading. You can see its hydraulic cylinders at work. The shelf in front protects the driver.

Inside the Cab

A giant dump truck has a tough job. It works in all kinds of weather. But the cab is very comfortable. It protects the driver. It keeps out noise and dust.

The cab has a big, comfortable seat. It has a steering wheel and a dashboard, just like a regular car. The cab has heat and **air-conditioning**. It even has a stereo. Drivers can listen to their favorite songs while they work!

The dashboard has many **gauges**. It has a computer screen, too. Computers give information about the truck and the load it carries. Drivers have to keep track of many things when a giant truck is working.

A driver steers his giant truck. While he drives, he checks the truck's computer screen. The ground is far below him!

At Work

Some mines produce coal. Other mines produce gold or silver. Many giant trucks work in coal mines. The coal is buried deep in the ground. Machines dig away dirt and rock to get it. The giant trucks take away the dirt and rock. Next, they take away the coal. Finally, they haul back the dirt and rock. Machines fill the hole.

The trucks are not very fast. But they never stop working. As soon as they drop off a load, they go back for more. They may have to drive on long hills. They work in rain and snow, heat and cold. They work at night, too.

This Euclid truck works in a mine. It is taking away rock and dirt. The giant shovel fills its bed very quickly!

Behind the Wheel

Before you drive, you walk around the truck. You check to see if everything is okay. Then you climb the long stairway to the cabin. You turn a key, just like in a car. The engine starts up.

Now comes the hard part. You are sitting very high. You cannot see much. You are not even sure where the wheels are! Safety is important. You have to watch for other people and machines. You park next to a shovel. The shovel loads you up, and you drive away. The ride is smooth for such a big truck.

Many hours later, you park. Another driver takes over. The truck keeps going!

A driver climbs to the cab. He is working at a mine. When the other truck is full, this truck will take its place. It is made by Dresser.

Truck Makers

Today, a few companies make the world's biggest electric trucks. These companies are Komatsu, Liebherr, and Terex. Liebherr makes the biggest truck. It is called the T 282B. It came out in 1999. It can carry a load that weighs more than two hundred cars!

These giant trucks are custom-built. Buyers tell the companies exactly what kind of truck they want. The companies ship all the pieces. Then they put the truck together at the job site. Many highway trucks are needed to ship just one giant truck. The trucks cost millions of dollars. A single tire costs more than most cars.

The trucks keep getting bigger. How big will they get?

This picture shows the inside of a Caterpillar factory.
A worker is checking the rear axle of a new truck.

More to Read and View

Books

C is for Construction: Big Trucks and Diggers from A to Z. Caterpillar (Chronicle Books)

Dump Trucks. Earth Movers (series). Joanne Randolph (PowerKids Press)

Dump Trucks. Mighty Movers (series). Sarah Tieck (Buddy Books)

I Drive a Dump Truck. Working Wheels (series). Sarah Bridges (Picture Window Books

Monster Road Builders. Angela Royston (Barron's)

Road Builders. B. G. Hennessy (Viking)

Videos

Big Job: The Biggest, Coolest Trucks Around (Discovery Communication)

Heavy Equipment Operator: Cranes, Dump Trucks, Dirt Movers and More What Do You Want to Be When You Grow Up (series) (Tapeworm)

I Dig Dirt (Big Kids Productions)

Let's Go See the Big Work Trucks (Blue Beetle)

Web Sites

Web sites change frequently, but we believe the following web sites are going to last. You can also use good search engines, such as **Yahooligans!** (www.yahooligans.com) or **Google** (www.google.com) to find more information about giant vehicles. Some keywords that will help you are *Caterpillar, diesel engines, dump trucks, giant trucks, Komatsu, Liebherr, mining trucks,* and *Terex.*

auto.howstuffworks.com/
    diesel1.htm
This web site shows how a diesel engine works.

science.howstuffworks.com/
    hydraulic.htm
Visit this web site to learn more about how hydraulic machines work.

www.cat.com/cda/layout?m=
    37840&x=7&location=drop
At this web site, you can see pictures of many big dump trucks made by Caterpillar, including the world's largest, the 797. Click "Off–Highway Trucks," then "797B".

www.liebherr.com/me/en/47597.asp
Liebherr makes many big mining trucks. At this web site, select a model, then click "images" to see pictures of giant Liebherr dump trucks.

www.terex.com/main.php?obj=
    prod&action=VIEW&id=19
This web page from the Terex web site has information about its giant dump trucks plus some pictures.

Glossary

You can find these words on the pages listed. Reading a word in a sentence helps you to understand it even better.

air-conditioning (**AIR-kun-dish-en-ing**): a system that keeps a place cool when it is hot outside. **14**

bed (**BED**): on a dump truck, the part that holds a load of material. **8, 12**

coal (**KOLE**): a black material made of long-dead plants. Coal is a fuel, and it is often used to power electric power plants. **4, 16**

cylinders (**SIL-in-durz**): tubes inside an engine where fuel explodes, giving the engine power. **10, 12**

diesel (**DEE-zull**): the name for a kind of engine and the special fuel it uses. Most diesel engines are very reliable. They often use less fuel than gas engines. **10**

fuel (**FYULE**): something that burns to provide energy. **8**

gauges (**GAY-jez**): devices that measure something, such as temperature. **14**

horsepower (**HORS-pow-ur**): the amount of power an engine makes, based on how much work one horse can do. **10**

hydraulic (**hi-DRAW-lick**): having to do with using water or another liquid to move something. **12**

mines (**MINES**): places where coal, gold, silver, and other things are taken out of the ground. Some mines are underground tunnels. Other mines are big holes, or pits. **4, 6, 16**

modified (**MOD-if-eyed**): made changes to something. **6**

radiators (**RAY-dee-ay-turz**): the parts in trucks and cars that help cool the engine. **10**

turbochargers (**TUR-boe-char-jurz**): machines that force more air into an engine, giving it more power. **10**

Index

air-conditioning 14
axle 20
beds 8, 12
cabs 8, 12, 14, 18
Caterpillar 4, 10, 20
coal 4, 16
cylinders 10, 12
dashboards 14
digging 4, 6
Dresser 18

electric motors 10
engines 8, 10, 18
Euclid 6, 16
fuel 8
gauges 14
gold 16
horsepower 10
hydraulic cylinders 12
Komatsu 20

Liebherr 12, 20
mines 4, 6, 16
off-highway trucks 4, 6
radiators 10
safety 18
seats 14
shovels 4, 16, 18
silver 16
steel 12

steering wheels 14
Terex 20
tires 8
turbochargers 10
wheels 10, 18